CELEBRATING THE FAMILY NAME OF TAYLOR

Celebrating the Family Name of Taylor

Walter the Educator

SKB
Silent King Books
a WhichHead Entertainment Imprint

Copyright © 2024 by Walter the Educator

All rights reserved. No part of this book may be reproduced in any manner whatsoever without written permission except in the case of brief quotations embodied in critical articles and reviews.

First Printing, 2024

Disclaimer

This book is a literary work; the story is not about specific persons, locations, situations, and/or circumstances unless mentioned in a historical context. Any resemblance to real persons, locations, situations, and/or circumstances is coincidental. This book is for entertainment and informational purposes only. The author and publisher offer this information without warranties expressed or implied. No matter the grounds, neither the author nor the publisher will be accountable for any losses, injuries, or other damages caused by the reader's use of this book. The use of this book acknowledges an understanding and acceptance of this disclaimer.

Celebrating the Family Name of Taylor is a memory book that belongs to the Celebrating Family Name Book Series by Walter the Educator. Collect them all and more books at WaltertheEducator.com

USE THE EXTRA SPACE TO DOCUMENT YOUR FAMILY MEMORIES THROUGHOUT THE YEARS

TAYLOR

In the heart of our name, there's a tale untold,

Celebrating the Family Name of
Taylor

A story that stretches from young to the old,

It echoes in the wind, in the whispering trees,

A name that flows through time like a river to seas.

The Taylors were weavers of cloth and of dreams,

Mending the seams of life's broken schemes,

Threading the needle through laughter and pain,

Crafting a fabric that withstands the rain.

From the hands of our elders, so steady and true,

A lineage was woven, in colors of blue,

With wisdom as warp and courage as weft,

Each thread was a choice, each choice a step.

They worked in the dawn and toiled in the night,

With eyes ever fixed on the future's bright light,

They built with their hands, but more with their hearts,

A tapestry of love in countless parts.

Celebrating the Family Name of

Taylor

In the fields of the past, where our ancestors trod,

Their feet carved a path on the fertile sod,

Their voices still echo in the halls of our mind,

Reminding us always to be gentle and kind.

The Taylors were not just in name, but in deed,

A family of strength, of honor, of creed,

They stood by each other, come joy or strife,

Binding their fates in the loom of life.

They spoke not of grandeur, of riches or fame,

But cherished the simple, the pure, the same,

In the warmth of a hearth, in the light of a smile,

They found their treasure, their reason, their style.

Through wars and through peace, through dark and through day,

The Taylors kept walking, come what may,

With shoulders together, they weathered the storm,

Celebrating the Family Name of

Taylor

For the family was shield, and love was their norm.

Now we stand on the shoulders of giants unseen,

Bearing the name like a banner serene,

And though time may change the world around,

In the name of Taylor, our roots are found.

Let the children remember, as the old ones did say,

That the Taylor name is a bright, steady ray,

It guides us, protects us, through life's winding road,

Celebrating the Family Name of

Taylor

In our hearts, the Taylor spirit is stowed.

ABOUT THE CREATOR

Walter the Educator is one of the pseudonyms for Walter Anderson. Formally educated in Chemistry, Business, and Education, he is an educator, an author, a diverse entrepreneur, and he is the son of a disabled war veteran. "Walter the Educator" shares his time between educating and creating. He holds interests and owns several creative projects that entertain, enlighten, enhance, and educate, hoping to inspire and motivate you. Follow, find new works, and stay up to date with Walter the Educator™ at WaltertheEducator.com

Milton Keynes UK
Ingram Content Group UK Ltd.
UKHW020048260824
447288UK00011B/311